OBOE CLASSICS
for the beginner

To access audio visit:
www.halleonard.com/mylibrary

Enter Code
4068-7394-4014-0553

ISBN 978-1-59615-358-5

MMO **Music Minus One**

EXCLUSIVELY DISTRIBUTED BY

HAL•LEONARD®

7777 W. BLUEMOUND RD. P.O. BOX 13819 MILWAUKEE, WI 53213

Visit Hal Leonard Online at
www.halleonard.com

Music Minus One

3411

OBOE CLASSICS
for the Beginner

4

Introduction to Volume 1

Dear Young Oboist and Teachers,

I compiled this collection with the Junior High or Middle School student in mind. Some students will be able to play the selections after one year of study; certainly after two years. The notes are easy, but the music is adult enough to be enjoyed life-long. A great deal can be learned by imitation; using your ear is the very best way to develop your concepts, but if you can't figure out how to reproduce something you hear, the booklet notes are here to show you my thought process. For example, a beautiful, shapely downward slur is far from a chance event! I hope this music will be fun for kids and helpful for teachers. I'd like to dedicate my work on this project to my teacher John Mack, who continues to challenge and inspire me and who instilled love and devotion for teaching. Thanks also to Gail Warnaar of The Double Reed Shop, Barnet, VT and David Hempel of Eble Music, Iowa City, IA for their time in helping me find and choose the repertoire of this series of recordings.

Sincerely,

Elaine Douvas

Franck - *Pièce V*

César Franck (1820-1890) was a French composer, a teacher at the Paris Conservatory, and a church organist for thirty-two years. Pièce V (pronounced "pee-ess sank") was originally one of his Five Pieces for Harmonium, a cousin of the organ. Try to bring out the mood of religious purity and nobility. A simple melody such as this (or any of the melodies in the Barret Oboe Method) is in danger of sounding "sing-song," that is, with a repetitious, monotonous accent on the beats. We must try hard to dignify the melody by bringing out the eighth notes between the beats broadly and melodically.

The tone should sound easy, sweet and flexible, with simple clarity and ring. It should sound aglow with a sort of inward animation and fragility. It's very important on the oboe that the lower the note, the deeper, longer, and more forest-colored the tone must be; and vice-versa, the high notes should become more brilliant and strong. As you progress downward from D to G in the first phrase, please make sure there is no shallowness of G compared with A. Make an exercise of this: A-G-A-G etc., making sure it goes "ee-oh-ee-oh," not "oh-aing-oh-aing." Bs and Cs are notoriously bare and thin on the oboe. Make an exercise of this too: B-C-B-C etc., trying to thicken and match the two tones and get a small half-step of pitch. Keep experimenting until the C is the same color as the B. Do it by ear, but you might try going to the tip of the reed, opening the jaws, and "overloading" or funneling extra air against the focus in the throat. The opposition of lipping down and wind-ing up gives breadth and content to the tone.

Making a graceful attack on the oboe is one of the first things you must master. We want the sound of forward motion in the attack, a nice flow like gently stepping onto a moving sidewalk at the airport without stopping to look at it and jolting on. It should be clear, with a sort of poetic emergence and finesse, and it should take nothing away from the tone. You take in your air, set your embouchure for stability, and put your tongue on the reed, just as string player would start with the bow on the string. We don't want to swat at the reed from a distance; that is too haphazard and uncontrolled. As you start to blow, pull the tongue away from the reed as the air is on the increase. Find just the right moment; if you wait too long and develop too much pressure, the attack will sound explosive.

Take care that the fingers move quietly, sneakily, curved, with a gentle squeezing action. Straight fingers can be heard as jagged, angular note changes. Try picking the fingers up a little before squeezing them down; if you keep them too close to the keys, the only way to get them down is to snap them. The oboe must cover well, so that the keys don't have to be hit for response.

Richard Strauss - *Zueignung (Dedication)*

In the last years of his 85-year-long life Richard Strauss wrote his Concerto for Oboe, one of the 3 or 4 most important solo works for our instrument. The more music you know by any composer, the more understanding you will bring to the rest of his works. When you are preparing any piece, listen to other examples by the same composer and look for similarities.

Zueignung (tsoo EYG noong) is a song for soprano and piano (later for orchestra) written when Strauss was only 18. It was his first published song. Has a more beautiful melody ever been written? The words tell of deep love, "...far from you I am in torment," "...you took away everything evil," and the quiet little refrain at the end of each verse, "Take my thanks" (the dotted 8th and 16th.) Whenever you play a piece that has words, it is essential to find out what is being said. In your interpretation try to express deep sincerity, urgency, and personal feeling. Try to convey soaring spirits

and elevation in the upward slurs. The tone will need to have fullness, body and sustaining power to match the rich accompaniment and to carry the seriousness and emotional weight of the music. Body must be built into the reed, and the reed must hold itself up to pitch so it doesn't have to be bitten. It is never too soon to make these concepts part of your goals for good tone. There is more technical advice on how to get this in the next paragraph about support in Gymnopédie.

Eric Satie - *Gymnopédie No. 3*

Satie wrote three Gymnopédies (pronounced "zhihm-no-pay-dee") for piano solo in 1888. The pieces were inspired by the figures painted on a Greek vase doing ceremonial athletic movements. Nos. 1 and 3 became famous oboe solos when the composer Debussy orchestrated them.

Satie was a strange and controversial man. He spent his whole career going against the musical establishment of his time; he hated Romanticism and Impressionism in music. He wrote lots of short piano pieces with humorous, sarcastic titles such as Three Pieces in the Form of a Pear and Desiccated Embryos! Satie's defenders believe that his conscious monotony expresses deeply concentrated thought. He has many admirers among the "minimalist" composers of the 1970s and 80s, such as John Adams and Philip Glass.

This piece would not make such a good contest piece, but if you practice it for smoothness, good support, excellent pitch, even tone quality and soft control, it will make everything you play better. The soft tone should sound open and ringing; it should not sound squeezed, bitten, muffled or missing its high overtones. Here is something to think about: support is not how much air you blow, but how you hold the air. To play softly, take a deep, medium breath (not every ounce of air you can fit in! no shoulders going up!) then control and concentrate the air by holding it firmly between the abdominal muscles and a place in the throat that focuses the tone. It's sort of like using your thumb over the end of the garden hose. If want to water the lowers 6 feet away, you wouldn't turn up the water full blast and knock all the petals off the flowers. You would keep the water amount moderate, and use your thumb to get a traveling, aerated stream. You can find this place in the throat by saying "young" (or by gargling!) You don't need much air to play the oboe, especially at this quiet volume. Blowing against yourself removes the sound of pressure at the reed, so it will sound clear, floating, elevated, pure and spare. There should be very little vibrato in this - - an exercise in simplicity.

Mary Chandler - *Three Dance Studies*

Mary Chandler's Three Dance Studies would make a great contest piece! The dance rhythms are "catchy" and very fun to play.

A habañera is a slow dance used in flamenco dancing; very sultry and provocative like the "Habañera" in Bizet's Carmen. Try to get "curve," that is, diminuendo in the syncopated notes; do not use a straight tone. After all, "syncopation" comes from the Latin "syncopare," which means "to faint or swoon." The notes should die away, so they will sound cool, haughty, aloof.

The Valse Sentimentale (in French "sahng-tee-mahng-tahl") is charming - - good practice for left D# and lightly sliding your index finger to clear the half-hole. When you tongue on the bar lines, try to get really smooth "bow changes" with no "hiccups" at the tonguing junctures. Tongue as late and fast as possible, and don't cut short the end of the note before the tongued one. Tongue clearly with "tee" or "tah," making sure that the tips of the reed are in the clear; no lip touching the tip! That makes blunt, popping attacks. The ratio of tone to tongue depends on the character of the music. In this case, we want mostly all tone and very little tongue. the tongue gently urges the tone forward like a smooth bow change. Think 98% tone to 2% tongue noise.

The Magyar, a lively Hungarian dance, needs lifts and spaces at the ends of the slurs. Lift them for rhythmic energy as if you sang an "m" syllable on the ends.

C. W. Gluck - *"What is Life?" from Orfeo ed Euridice*

It's always fun to play a piece that has a story. "What is Life Without Euridice?" (Italian: "Che Faro senza Euridice?") is the full title here. The song is from the last act of Gluck's opera Orpheus and Euridice, written in 1762. The story is based on the Greek myth where Orpheus makes a deal with the gods that he can bring his wife, Euridice (yoo RIH dih chee) back from the dead on condition that he not look at her during the long journey through the forest back to the land of the living. Euridice is so upset, confused and begging, that Orpheus finally looks, and she is lost to him again. In this song he entreats the gods to bring her back. He is so persuasive and so poignant that the god of love, Amor, is moved to pity, brings her back to life and the opera ends happily.

There are speech-like sections in this called "recitative" (rech ih tuh TEEV) that have very flexible tempo and are meant to sound dramatic and rhetorical. Try to hear a recording of a great mezzo-soprano singing this so you can learn to play vocally, imitating the curves and inflections of speech and the variety of consonant sounds. Orpheus is sung by a mezzo-soprano so he will sound very youthful.

The high notes need to be big, spacious, broad and full; not tiny, bitten, thin or squeezed. Try rolling a little more lips and reed together into your mouth. This will get the pitch up by position on the reed, so that you can voice downward in the throat for depth and aeration. You will have to be able to shift back out the tip for the middle and low registers. When you practice scales try to make a habit of counteracting the oboe's tendency to sound loud in the low notes and thin in the high notes. Start very softly in the low register, crescendo to the fullest at the top of the scale, and diminuendo again to the bottom. That's the way a voice sings; it's the natural way of music.

·aditional - *Greensleeves / Lovely Joan*

These two English melodies have been around since the Middle Ages. Strive for ıoothness of air and fingers (curved.) Let the melodies crescendo when they go up ıd diminuendo when they go down. Take care that low G is deeper than A. Try not interrupt the forward flow of the line with too much tongue; tongue late and fast ithout ending the previous note. If you cultivate really noiseless, fluent breathing, en you can breathe as often as you like without chopping up the music. Be sure to ace the dotted rhythm properly, especially the eighth notes on beats 3 and 6. The cteenth note can be either brought out (when its an upper neighbor) or played late ıd flexibly (when it's a passing tone or a lower neighbor.) Whether to lilt or sustain ·pends on how serious the mood is. Some of each is okay here. In Lovely Joan, be re the little notes are well sustained and do not drop out of the line. Play the 8th ıte after the dotted quarter very generously; not late, not weak, not clipped. amless tonguing is needed here too.

dvard Grieg - *Norwegian Dance op. 35 no. 2*

Grieg is Norway's most famous composer. He studied in Germany, developed an ternational style, and wrote some large-scale works such as his famous Piano Concerto a minor and The Peer Gynt Suite (for further listening.) He always loved the folk ngs of his native country, and by setting them for full orchestra he dignified and ımortalized many of them. This dance, written in 1881, is a big oboe solo in the full chestra version. The mood should be quiet, poised, and graceful with a nice lift on the ›ward swings of the melody. The upbeat sixteenth note in the dotted rhythm should be ry precisely placed, short and accented. The staccato dots at the end of a slur mean to t the end of the slur, not to tongue the note. The grace notes in m. 18 and 20 should ıitate the sound of the harp "rolling a chord" in the orchestra version - - very graceful.

The middle section should be fiery and sturdy; not too fast. Try to get a lot of ıg in the repeated Es with good outline on the tone. The interesting contrast of oods makes this a wonderful contest piece.

éo Delibes - *"Flower Duet" from Lakmé*

The opera Lakmé (lahk may) was written in 1883. Lakmé is the daughter of a ndu priest during the mid-1800s when India was being colonized by the British. .kmé falls in love with her country's enemy, a British officer named Gerald. ıings don't turn well: her father stabs Gerald, then she sneaks him away to an and to nurse him back to health. When she realizes that he feels loyalty to his giment, Lakmé eats a poison flower and dies, telling Gerald that he has given her he sweetest dream under heaven."

The "Flower Duet" is sung by Lakmé and her slave at the beginning of the opera they stand at the water's edge preparing to bathe. She leaves her dazzling jewels on bench where Gerald will happen onto them, fascinated. The two ladies leave in a ıat. The music is a "barcarolle," that is, a boat song in 6/8 rhythm. It should have a ntle rocking motion, elegance and vocal style. Instrumentalists should always try to ay in the way that singers sing. There are many things that go into this, and here e the first two: 1) "legato" or smoothness, lack of mechanical interference (such as ys clicking) on note changes. 2) shapely slurs: a slight scoop shape when going up, slight arch on downward slurs.

The downward slurs here can be difficult. They must be active slurs; don't just let em drop out! Try aiming upward instead of straight down at the note. The shape ould be arched as if going over a waterfall: out first, then down. Bring the air to a est at the end of the upper note then, at the last moment before changing notes, actically stop blowing as you go to the lower note. This gets a lot of content in the terval or "portamento" (Italian for "carried over,") and it is very vocal.

I would suggest tonguing the grace-note in the last line. Indeed, most grace-ıtes sound better tongued for clarity, because they are harmonically interesting, ıd to prevent them from sounding like a dotted rhythm.

uigi Boccherini - *Minuet*

This famous melody is very stylish and fun to play. It comes from the days of ›wdered wigs, and it should sound like an elegant party, very happy and full of ring in the dance rhythm. There are lots of high As, however, and this can be a flat, ıstable note on the oboe. The best guarantee of stability on high A is to have a good itch floor" built into the reed. When the reed holds itself up to pitch you can actu-ly voice down on the high notes for fullness, keeping the jaws apart. Hold this ought until the day when you start to make your own reeds. (Pitch floor is a func-ın of tight sides and some "stoppage" behind a tip that is not too long.) Try for lots ring in the octave As on pg. 2. It will help if you roll in a bit more lips and reed gether. Then the high notes will not sound pressured by jamming them up with ur wind or biting. Let all the syncopations "die away," and lift the 8th notes (not the 3ths) at the ends of the slurs to match the short notes that follow. I recommend arting the C# - B trill with the full C# fingering, and then switch to the trill key.

ichard Wagner - *"Walther's Prize Song" from Die Meistersinger*

Here is another beautiful song with an inspiring story from the comic opera ie Meistersinger. The "Mastersingers" were poet-troubadours, knights of the 500s. You know the type: going from town to town, singing serenades under dies' balconies, saving damsels in distress.

Walther (VAHL ter) is a stranger, newly arrived in town. He falls in love with ra, the most beautiful maiden, only to find out that her father has promised her hand marriage to the winner of a song contest tomorrow. The song contest is only open "Masters of the Guild," a sort of union. Walther is a fine poet and singer and a sen-ive, expressive youth, but he simply doesn't know all the rules for song-writing cording to the Guild. (Wagner was poking fun at his own critics who said he didn't know the rules!) The Prize Song comes to Walther first in a dream. A kindly older Mastersinger helps him fix it up to meet the rules.

The scene of the song contest is very exciting: an open meadow by a river, big parade, lots of banners, the townsfolk all in festive dress, cheering. Eva is very nervous because she wants Walther to win and marry her. After a very funny attempt by a little professor named Beckmesser, Walther gets his chance. In a mood of great reverence, this song tells his vision of a lovely garden in which he has found the most beautiful maiden in the world, Eva. The townsfolk are deeply moved, the Mastersingers declare him the winner, and Eva puts her laurel wreath on his head singing, (in the last 8 bars of the arrangement here) "No one could have deserved it more."

In playing the melody, I'm sure you can feel the expression and stress on m. 2, the dissonant E, resolving to D. Always bring out this feeling of stress and relief, and don't play all the notes with the same intensity. This dissonance has a name: the E is an "appoggiatura," (uh pojya TOO ruh) that is, a note that doesn't fit with the chord of the moment, but it pulls strongly to the neighboring note that is in the harmony. We play these dissonances with expression and emphasis, then the resolution is felt as relief, repose. Ordinarily you would neither blow harder nor bite to play softly; there is no repose in that! To play softly, blow less air and adjust the "thumb over the garden hose" in your throat to keep the travel and compression in the tone. Don't bite the reed or it will lose it's color and ring, it won't respond to a smaller amount of air, and you'll be sharp on all of your diminuendos.

Be sure to sustain the dotted quarters; it is very important to connect the long notes with the start of the moving notes. Do not make a habit of lilting away from the long notes! A slur is not a "phrase mark," just a smooth "bow-change," gently urging the tone forward. Make beautiful, arch-shaped downward slurs: over the waterfall, out first, then down.

César Cui - *Orientale*

César Cui (kyoo EE) (1835-1918) was a Russian composer, the least famous of the so-called "Mighty Handful" that included Rimsky-Korsakov, Mussorgsky, Borodin and Balakirev. All of these men earned their living in non-musical fields: in the Army, the Navy, as engineers and scientists. Although he wrote ten operas and over 300 songs, Cui never gave up his career as an engineering officer and professor of fortifications!

Orientalism in music was extremely popular at the turn of the century, and the oboe, with its "snake-charmer" associations, always figures prominently in exotic music, such as Rimsky-Korsakov's Scheherazade, the "Arabian Dance" from Tchaikowsky's Nutcracker and Ibert's Escales. Read the sharps and flats accurately and enjoy the "exotic intervals" C#-Bb and Eb-F# (augmented seconds.)

The mood of Orientale is similar to the habañera: cool, aloof, sneaky, subtle. Be sure to stress the Bb on m. 2 and diminish to the long G. Don't let the longer notes stick out just because they're long - - that's "accidental syncopation." "Con morbidezza" means "with morbidity." Always look up the words you don't know! Try my recipe for downward slurs (see "Flower Duet") so you can get a soft low D. Keep the fingers curved and quiet. A word about vibrato: it should confirm, not confuse the pitch and stay within the tone outline. Vibrato is a gentle waving of the vocal chords, a sort of loud-soft pulsation more than a pitch change. It is not supposed to make any noise in the throat.

William Walton - *Three Pieces from Richard III*

Sir William Walton (1902-1983) was an English composer who wrote the background music for lots of classic English films including the 1955 Richard III by Shakespeare. If you like Shakespeare, see this; it's great! Lawrence Olivier directed and stars as the evil, deformed king who kills 11 people to get to the throne!

The "March" and the "Scherzetto" (skairt ZETTO) both occur near the beginning as coronation music for Edward IV. The mood is joyous, regal, heroic, and full of rhythmic energy. The oboe should sound trumpet-like. We want good articulation that takes nothing away from the tone; think 95% tone to 5% attack. Be sure the tips of the reed are in the clear with no lip on the tip, or you will get blunt, popping attacks. Use the tip of your tongue directly into the reed's opening. Practice staccato notes on the reed alone to get rid of any pitch changes and any double sounds in the start or end of the note.

The "Elegy" occurs when Edward IV is on his deathbed (a rare instance of death by natural causes!) He begs all of the nobles to make peace with each other and embrace. His wife, Elizabeth, declares it a "holy day" and hopes for better times ahead. (It only gets worse, as 8 murders are still to come!)

This is good practice for counting the mixed meters. Just remember that a quarter note always has the same beat, there are just different numbers of them in each bar. In the first 8 bars, crescendo a little toward the ties on the 3rd beats, a point of harmonic tension (a "suspension,") followed by relief.

We chose to play the "March" and the "Scherzetto" faster than the printed metronome marks. Metronome marks are often by an editor rather than the composer, and you must use your own good judgment.

William Walton - *"Trumpet Tune" from Children's Suite*

There are 8 short pieces in Walton's Children's Suite; "Trumpet Tune" is no. 8. It is a piece of interesting contrasts and would, therefore, make a good contest solo. "Quasi tromba" means "like a trumpet," so play in an out-going, exuberant way, like a fanfare with clean, clear tonguing. On the pairs of 8th notes, try to play two distinct, equally short notes! I refer you to Barret Oboe Method melodies 11, 12 and 13 to practice this. For the quarters, you should elongate the ones that have 2 eighth notes following. The smooth middle section is marked "gracefully expressive." If the notes go up, crescendo; if they go down, get softer. You can play the upper octave at m.51-59 if you want practice playing high Eb and Db!

Cesar Franck
Pièce V

3411

Richard Strauss
Zueignung

3411

Eric Satie
Gymnopédie No. 3

Mary Chandler
Three Dance Studies
Habanera

Valse Sentimentale

Magyar

C.W.Gluck
What Is Life?

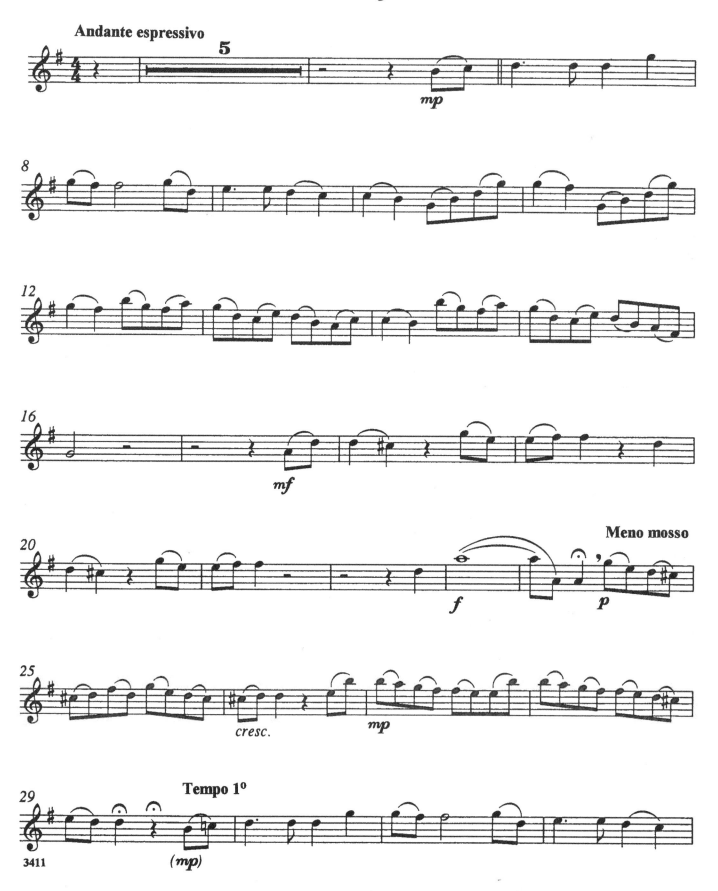

Traditional
Greensleeves/Lovely Joan

Edvard Grieg
Norwegian Dance

3411

Leo Delibes
Flower Duet (Lakmé)

Boccherini
Minuet

D. 𝄋 al Coda

3411

Wagner
Walther's Prize Song

César Cui
Orientale

Op.50

3411

Walton
3 Pieces from Richard III
March

3411

Three Pieces from 'Richard III' from an Oboe Album by William Walton.
Arranged by Christopher Palmer. © Oxford University Press 1992.

Walton
Elegy

Walton
Scherzetto

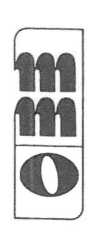

Walton
Trumpet Tune

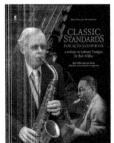

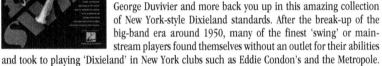